"Children Lie; I Did..."

poems, passages & a broken kite.

mehjabin h. prova

For permission requests, write to the publisher, addressed "Attention: Permissions Coordinator," at the email address below.

ISBN (Paperback): 9798367934168
ISBN (Hardcover): 9798367941906

Imprint: Independently Published
Email: oeuvre.publications@gmail.com

Cover Artist: Mehjabin H. Prova
Library of Congress Control Number: 2022903934
Printed in the United States of America & Germany

For all of us who grew up feeling helpless, without any emotional comfort:

"If once we could stand alone in the dark, it's alright to stand alone in the light as well."

Table of Contents:

INTRODUCTION

The kite I had is missing — whether it's broken, whether it's unseen for the night in the sky, or if it's just playing hide and seek with me — I sure don't know its whereabouts. But it never takes an unannounced flight again… is my only wish now.

This place I lie is thousands of feet beneath the clouds I touch, and it's not gravity that pulls me down here, it's the string that kite left tangled around me. It gets harder to breathe, as if this string I'm entangled in pulls me further beneath the ground to search for all the corpses I left when I died but it finds yet another chance to dig a grave deeper.

An impure state I've been lured into only calls for the wolves, ravens and serpents — devious enemies of their own and envious of who gets to me first. Will this hyacinth ingrown in me be another hopeless attempt to return me to my kite? Is it just a fragrance that's still rearing in me to only invite the unknown? For the person who I aspire to be, if one day I catch my kite, will it ever let go of me?

Children think of such questions, don't they? I did, but they were simpler in my mind. Now, I'm not sure whether it's because I've grown up or if it's because I'm growing older, but it all sounds as if I'm speaking a foreign language to myself. Today for the world I speak only a few languages but for me, I've self-learnt and spoken the language of love, resent, violence, hope, sorrow, and gentleness; and to cover them all I've mastered the language of lies. *Lies* — a universal language known to be misused by many but, for some it's the only weapon that was used to save them.

CHASING

Reaper Train

Chasing along the tracks to visit me had come a train from somewhere far ahead in time. Just as I had expected, the date it arrived at my station was truly unexpected. Even though I wasn't really aware of what it had run over while rushing to me, I accepted its invitation. "Take me with you, I'll be your passenger sooner or later."

Now that I look back, it's too late to say it but I said that in a haste for still holding a grudge — the so-called ticket — against myself for the past which had nonetheless chased me all along. It stopped at countless stations for several others, however, none of us could foretell what the next station would bring. None of us could foresee what would be on its tracks waiting to be stamped out, waiting to be overcome.

"I've lived enough, haven't I?" — with this ridiculously invalid reason of mine, I wondered if anyone else had got on with the same ticket as me, but later I genuinely hoped otherwise. Will I be getting off any time soon? What's the point though? Now that I've put my feet on it, getting off would be a journey just too short; and this grudge I hold is still holding me back from regretting a brief life.

Would I get another chance to witness one more who's willing like me? Maybe to be honest, I was just looking for an assurance that I wasn't the only one making this mistake. But there's nothing to worry about since I never witnessed the reassurance I sought.

Out of my boredom from this long, lonely journey, I speculated on why there were ones who were unwilling to be a passenger of this reaper train from the future. And though there were many outcomes before each station, at the end of my journey I figured: In this instance, we're all still dead in a future that is yet left to be formed. For all that it's worth, reaching my terminal led me to a question for all those who are naively willing to make the same mistake as mine — why would you willingly kill yourself twice?

Orbit

I’ve been all around the world.
Concrete cities, tavern towns,
hollow people, colours all around.

But neither can I forget you
nor do I find a way back to you.
What’s the point of chasing?

I keep orbiting the same route
knowing damn well there are others
fiercely running the same ground.

Apparently, others have it much worse than me. Others, unsurprisingly so, have a much more miserable life than I do. But if I must be honest, it kind of sucks to know this. It really infuriates me at times to be aware of how there are millions of people going through a life that could easily be compared to hell. My awareness plays with my sanity, because I know I won't be able to justify my weaknesses the same way anymore. Because every time I'm on the verge of convincing myself of being the most miserable person to exist, I tell myself: "At least I'm sure I smiled once today." And if I haven't yet smiled by that moment, I smile, and go on to say it to myself anyways.

Run Away

If you want to run away
just to find your own peace
you will never succeed
to escape it for good.

Without overthinking
about the outcome,
sort out the issue or
bring it under control.

Whether good or bad,
whether peace or war,
you have to live with it all
and move forward anyway.

That's not how life should be,
but that is how it is.

Race

Why do I like you?
What could it be that made me
obsess over someone so vague?

I didn't even know your name.
But there I was trying to give it a reason.
And by the end of each day,
I still had nothing to say.
If someone asked, my mind would race
to point out a cause too twisted…
if one day it was how you hid your tears,
the next I would say it was
how you always remained at sight.

And still, by the end of every one of those
conversations, I would return to
question myself: why do I like you?

Search

When people ask me about myself, I get taken aback by the realisation, *I don't know who I am.* Along the way of searching for my identity, I guess I have also lost the least that I had known of myself.

So, it's not always true when adults make us believe that through the process of growing up from a child to being them, we have to know who we might become. It's not always true that being a careless, rebellious teenager will lead us to become nothing but mediocre, and it's not always true that being a quiet, well-mannered kid will lead us to reach heights without even pursuing after them. It's not always true that playing against the rules will lead us to be morally improper; and it's not always true that walking in a straight line will lead us to the right destination.

What leads us to live the happiest of our times?
No one has grown to live that depiction of perfect happiness; no one will. Growing up is what we must do without knowing we are, and only then we can feel every part of life and feel ourselves change without having to label every version of who we are. Stop the search.

Defence Mechanism

I've watched my father cry way too less, and my mother cry her life away. Time doesn't really fly by when it's needed; I often watch myself do nothing but sit still until I'm done being consumed by the stranded silence that only calls for me to let it all out. The uncountable ways of dealing with problems that I have observed along the marathon of growing up has succeeded to influence me to a point where I seem to use a method that is just in-between them all.

Light

I will chase the flickers of
light you always leave behind.
No matter which way you drive,
I want to be right beside.
No need to change our paths,
let's just wait for what we find.

HOPELESS

Assure You

I assure you; I wrote this one just for you. Since I know, you won't ever bother to read into it or ever see the depth of my *'meaningless'* words, let's just let the world witness:
"I do assure you; I know how to ease your mind.", that's what I whispered (to myself) when I noticed your hands tremble restlessly every now and then, at every glimpse. Trust me, I knew keeping her by your side after every little fight had kept you up at night.

"Those memories you had to cage inside; I know it's not easy to let someone in to find." Do you remember that field of faded dandelions where you broke down on your knees? I never asked what was wrong, but did you ever ask how I knew? You were like a hopeless romantic for her, just as I was for you.
"I'll surely let you be the one to decide.", a sentence that broke both our hearts. The difference was: I said it to myself, while you had to say it to her.

"But hey, sometimes it gets tiresome to be the only one always being there." Our first fight had rooted from that. But to be honest, at times it really did get difficult to ease your mind as a friend. Then again, if you weren't there for me as something as simple as a friend, how could I expect anything more?
"Hey, I'll try to be patient… even when at times it feels a bit unfair." I never spoke the words after *'patient'* though; I just needed to apologise and make it up to you. Foolish, I know.

"I do assure you; I'll make myself know how to be by your side.", being blind in love and immature, I had tried to convince us both how I would become another version of you. Yet again, just to ease the trouble to your mind I promised, "Otherwise, it's alright. I've always been prepared to leave my heart confined."

"Those lies which fooled you into opening your heart that wide, I know it's not easy to forget the scars someone else just left behind." All these pathetic sympathies I showed, they were not enough to get through to you. But somehow, ironically, they were enough for me to turn into another you.

Goodbye

You joked it's not the last day
that I'll have you coming by.
But that expression on your face
had left me wondering why…
Why did it look like
a purposely unsaid goodbye?

You were hers; I was yours — that's how we started,
and that's exactly how we parted.

Once Again

Could you dream of me a little?
Once, just as I do of you.

Just as we witness the sky being so blue,
my heart and mind still belong to you.

Was your song written for her?
Again, like the ones I had composed for you.

You break my heart and I write it all down,
like it's the most beautiful poem ever.

One Gets Burned

What is a romance without love?
Flames of lust,
curtained beneath a lace of
no expectations,
no commitments,
no heartbreaks –
unless of course, one of them
starts to get *burned*.

Intricate Creatures

I hopelessly tried to make ‘us’
happen, knowing damn well that
I would be the first one to back off.
Human beings are intricate creatures
and at a particular point of what
has now become history,
I certainly forced myself to be
more complex than I already was.

The red light has passed a couple times so far, but I still stand here before the crossway… and I ask myself all over again: *"Haven't I lost my chance already?"* Cars have slowed down, flashing lights on this bleak avenue are still and motionless — that red light has arrived once again, but my feet won't walk through this path anymore which is drenched for the heart that leaks in your name without a bloodstain.

INSPIRATION

Commitments Burnout

He tends to set things on flames, then leave with the extinguisher. “Staying to watch whether it will easily burnout or, set a bigger fire isn’t what I do.”, was a statement he had told me once. By the majority, he had been misunderstood – that he was mature enough to not look back and easily move on, live forward without a care for the outcome.

“Is that not what he implied?”

“Probably.”

But what time has perceived of him is now much different; he proved to be a figure far from someone I would look up to. He can be the cause of the fire, yes, but what he does afterwards is a result of his impatient, uncommitted, and irresponsible personality. Causing the fire and being the reason of the fire may be ultimately distinct, however, being uncommitted and being irresponsible are equally indistinguishable.

Let Me Down

Was I deceived by those
broken pieces
you mended with gold?
Cause every time
I look at you now,
things go wrong
just as if they were
destined to let me down.

You did trust me; I won’t deny that.
But just not when I needed it the most.

Older

Do you ever get heartbroken by yourself? That moment when you realise your unbendable stubborn habits changed all of a sudden. When you realise you can't forgive yourself for burying the 'older' you deep within. When you realise, you're about to lose everything and it's never going to be the same; it's never coming back. When you realise how lonely you've made yourself just for the sake of letting out all your anger. Just one unexpected storm, and you've let yourself forget who you are.

Either way they're gonna judge me, so why don't I let them judge me the way I want? As long as I am honest with myself and don't force myself to be just as perfect as I envision myself to become one day, there's nothing to be afraid of.

Feeling You

How does it feel to be you —
I wonder.
I wonder how it feels
to be loved by me.
I wish I could feel
that love for myself too.
I wish for me,
I could be an inspiration too.
How does it feel to be you —
I wonder.
I wonder how it feels
to be admired by me.
I wish I could feel
that admiration for myself too.
Once in a while I wish,
I could be an inspiration for you.

Liar of Light

He was a shadow that illuminated a gleam of light to my eyes but, the closer I reached, his overpowering dusk began to show itself. The light was not his, but of someone unknown who was miles away. Just like a star, he hid his true self — deceiving all those who looked up to him.

The biggest hypocrites you'll ever know, at most times turn out to be the ones closest to you.

Regret comes in many ways; however, the difference remains in the outcome. Without an attempt, there's no outcome. With attempt, there's at least the satisfaction of trying no matter the outcome. And attempting it halfway, is topping the regret with frustration and self-rejection.

LAIN

There She Was

And there she was: entering through the doorsteps carrying a steely breeze of the colourless morning; her eyes draped with the sadness of the moon being withered away and her lips dusted with the sealed burgeons of last sunset's hibiscuses.

But her reflection on the mirror mimicked what others around her had portrayed: a prideful crested bulbul who sings an aubade to be predated upon by lovers, a lone leopard who shows to be extravagant – just an unusual tactic used to hunt for her prey; and an overwhelming blossom of oleanders which could be a silent killer in disguise.

Something so fragile and fragrant as a Persian lime turns bitter when it's bruised, sour when it's crushed, sere when it's abandoned; and she was nothing less unlike when it came to being viewed violently and used unjustly. There she was, lain beneath that coarsely undefined surface.

Necessity

Blood —
you see, is a necessity.
For it to run in our veins it makes us living,
for it to be feminine it makes us be born,
and for it to bleed us out it makes us die.
Blood —
a thirst that is trapped,
a thirst that is quenched,
and a necessity made of us
to only rest within us.

Aster

You should really be my disaster.
Bring out all my imperfections
before they become engraved
lain beneath my deceitful image.
Bring forth all my tears of aster,
before I make them wash away
with the ales of wisdom and sage.
You should really be my disaster
before I become my own detester.

Normally Mad

What's this all for? *"Has she gone mad?"*, you might be thinking. But whoever you are, let me tell you something, I was never *not* mad. If you ever see me and think whatever I'm doing is normal, that's probably when I've gone truthfully mad. And whoever I am, I try my utmost best to not get myself hurt to that extent… but at times, I end up being hurt anyways. Honestly though, *what is this all for?* I asked myself as well. Why am I writing all of this out loud? All of these lies, all of these honest words, all the time in the world to be honestly happy, and still ending up miserably hurt.

You

This nameless gloomy place I'm lying at,
don't you hear
how it's been calling for you?
Those heavy clouds over my head,
can't you feel
them crying to thunder for you?
These drenched dark wings I have,
can't you see
how lonely they are without you?
That nostalgic blue sky I had,
don't you know
it's been longing for me to fly with you?

Conifers

Lying beneath a meeting of silently breathing conifers, I looked up. And I found myself lain still, wrapped within a fine string of the kite which had now been blown away. I'm not sure whether it was the moon I saw for that brief second — glowing luminance, white streaks, hidden grey spots of scars — all in just those couple blinks I could take. I couldn't feel the earth beneath me, or the dewy grass surrounding me; none of my limbs seemed to reach the sense of those feelings. But it was that crawling sensation, like a phantom on my skin, of those tiny, loosened threads that made me aware of being alive. How could that stringless kite escape the conifers? And how could I not?

How can I of all, be afraid of the dark? It has been my home no matter how far I look back.

Terminal

One lies facing the sea of blankness
projecting all that shouldn't have been,
one lies on a defeated pillow still absorbing
more tears than it already soaked in.
The last stage of someone's
sadness and grief are their tears.
But before being faced with that terminal,
one first goes past all their fears.

Heirloom

In how many families do children inherit generational heirlooms? And in how many do they also inherit generational melancholia? Do those children ever have the option to deny that unwanted legacy? My grandparents were the heirs to their parents' melancholy, my parents inherited the heavy hearts of their generations before; and here I lie on a pillow that weighs the mass of those several generations before me. As a fact, not a single generation goes by without observing their elders inherit it too. Will this heirloom called *melancholia* ever stop being passed on? The generations after me will tell, if and only if they're no more unknown like the trauma that rooted us all to be here.

DEAD

Broken Marble

Does the Dead Sea dare to defy the demons who reside on that damaged sphere dominating its stolen light? A broken marble is all that it is, and it survives only for the night praised by a few. And what is life beyond that visibly bruised marble? Our world — just another broken little marble revolving perfectly on its own orbit that begins and ends on the same path but barely touches the sun — a marvel. Even if they're both chipped in different ways, they keep on chasing their set destination until they either reach their objective or at one point entirely disintegrates. Broken, but still carrying on without a care for its injuries just like the beings on it, as if we are all in a game of breaking and making — playing long enough to end up beside the demons which reside on the moon to be forgotten quite often. And only those that can look upon that lunar reflection on the Dead Sea know how in the scramble for making something of ourselves we keep ignoring how broken we become along the way.

Moorland

In this compellingly callous
midwinter drizzle,
my drenched heart feels untamed and
too selfishly driven to not let you go.

I stand, praying to God I don't lose
this barely begun bond:
"Could the billowing clouds not take you away?"

Now I still stand here
for another year, another day:
As I'm back on this
moorland,

the spiralling pain rips through
like a crooked cold chisel…
"Those ghastly grey skies still stole you away."

Corpse

There's no point in saving me…
I've been hurt a times too many.

If there was a corpse

every time I died internally,
the world would turn into a cemetery.

Last Breath

She was a museum of all his thoughts and memories framed by their feelings. She had made up her mind:

"Every drop of tear that I shed will cost me a memory. I can't cry; not for him. Not if he must live on, in my mind."

— until her last breath, he lived on.

Just one minute of standing in complete isolation and serenity, I had witnessed the forest grow with more desperation to let go of its hesitation and dance with the winds; I witnessed the moonless sky filled with clouds which looked more like cigarette smog emitting a grey radiance to befriend my shadow. I witnessed the stars become obscure with a sudden rush of the winds and I also witnessed that hesitation run back to make them still. Just one minute made me witness a whole new feeling of the living. And just how many more minutes do we live?

Deserted

How do you go
from being someone’s
everything, heart, and bones…
to being beyond invisible
than death –
like aimlessly swirling
within a deserted storm?

A Life

I must be out of my mind
to look for warmth
in this cricketing summer.
I must be out of my mind
to like black and white in a world
bustling with the prettiest colours.
I must be out of my mind
to search for a life standing
within a crowd and a city of clutter.

Save Me

Save me from myself;
pull me out of the water!
I don't dare to kill myself;
I can't break myself for any better.
Wherever I belong I'm still not there.
Strings and bones — they're black and blue.
I've loved a world that never treated me fair.
With the pain that we all went through,
I know I shouldn't dare to compare.
But I can't hold onto this dismantling sledge —
how do I entrust me to myself again when not
pulling the trigger pushes me towards the edge?

Survivor

You’re pretty when you’re dead:
Skin flushed like roses on pearls of white
and the fingers once held became cruelly dry.
Your lips — they’re colder than a glacier
but the blood on them tastes a lot warmer.
This sharp flavour of metal within a humid cell —
it was in those hands but I, I drove it through.
You’re pretty when you’re dead, can’t you tell?

I have life in me, and I have death in me.
What I don't have,
is the courage to continue either.

Rumination

Love has disappointed me for sure, but it disappointed me way less than my childhood did. Love — I can bear to live once more, but my childhood? Sometimes even going six feet under seems easier than living it all over again.

Living Dead

We all survive in a graveyard of the living:
some of our dreams die to push us back to nowhere,
while others die to give life to ambitions.
We all survive in a cemetery of dead desires:
some of our desires die to remind us of who we are,
while others die to let go of our superstitions.
We all survive in a memorial that is only of us living.

REARING

Sidereus & Stellifer

I miss you. I miss you so so much, that the craziness of it all has altered how I comprehend what I perceive. Peace can only exist after chaos has played its part. Light can only exist in the presence of dark. Is that why you and I had to break out hearts apart?

Benevolent Darkness

When the moon hides away with dawn,
I wonder whether my sorrows will disappear.

Shadows lurk in the dark to deceive a fawn.
Yet, they fail to draw me away from my fear.

Even in a battlefield of the silver powered
I remain nothing but a used hapless pawn.

I wonder whether there's still a light to be drawn
within the benevolent darkness that I rear.

One thing leads to another: and we're back to being in despair again. Momentary unhappiness, sniffles of affection, carelessly unnoticed blessings, and a home of loneliness — they're just part of the dystopian loop of despair no one can seem to escape.

Wanderer

Does your mind wander too often? To think that every time you said something, your words could've been too harsh or too deceptive.

Does your mind ever wander off? To think that sometimes, some words that you don't even remember saying could end up being the very reason for someone to get their hopes up or get their souls crushed.

Does your mind wander too often? To think that every time you did something, your acts had made someone think of you differently.

Does your mind ever wander off? To think that sometimes, some actions that you didn't even bother to think through could end up making someone misinterpret your motives.

Something so beautiful that makes you fall in love, can indeed have a heart erupting reason behind its beauty.

Secrets

All the secrets I bear could be
stamped on all these pages,
and even more.

But how fortunate for you
that I keep on saying less,
and a lot lesser.

How fortunate for you that
I mention only those distinctive details,
and one less burdensome feature.

Would drawing a line between us make it easier to step back from the edge?

The Liar

When did the child rearing in me begin to die? When was it, that child stopped speaking of what came to mind? When was it that child stopped loving freely, and create chaos? When was it that child hid behind a taller, darker, and sulkier shadow? Only a few know while many don't, and I remain among none of them because this shadow I am, pretends not to know.

If my love must be compared to something, compare it to all the seas on earth, and the space which is beyond all the stars we perceive.

Paragon

Born in the womb of an artist,
how would I rear anything
less than the masterpiece she created?
The colours I had consumed in her
makes me who I am, she's my painter.

Slates of blues, mosses of greens,
spectrums of beiges, ashes of greys,
and even ruins of charcoals —
what could I be if not a paragon
of a contemplative workmanship?

Bones

These bones I harness cages the feeble.
I'm heavily guarded, but only by myself:
I have no weapons; I know no violence.
It's just me and these bones that I harness.

We look up to the stars to guide us, but what if that star itself is aimless among its own boundless sky?

Explore & Explode

I remember how little me
wanted to be an astronaut:
see the stars up close,
touch the moon then
watch the earth revolve below.

And not long after,
I also remember watching
my dreams get crushed
down by an asteroid.

The universe is
where my dreams explore,
and it is where my dreams explode.

ENVIOUS

Position & Possession

To be brutally, violently honest, I envy your kind. While you lead the world pretending to be our shields, in reality we are just systematised to become nobodies under your shadows. After all, we are nothing but women, right? A kind dissimilar to yours, which you tend to see as a position and a possession lower than being a human being. You can pretend to not hear us until you need the sweetness of our comforting words. You can pretend to not see us until you are after a body that can fulfil your crude desires. You can pretend we don't exist until you need our remains to put on a show of your bravery for guarding and protecting us.

We are all human beings, until we are women. Would you care to give me an antidote to this unlawful parasite of enviousness?

A few weeks ago, one of our kind had been burned to death for running away from an illegal arrangement of marriage. No one was charged, but the prideful old groom received compensation for not having a bride to wed. Few days ago, one had been framed by her husband as a cheater just because none of their children were born as males. Their daughters were left fatherless, but the ungrateful husband received an alimony worth a hundred acres which he'd spend on his new wife. And a few moments ago, one of us were denied filing a lawsuit because she would *'most probably lose'* for the way she dressed. She was asked to remove her scarf to be identified, but now her assaulter roams free in a new hunt for another one of our kind that you call women.

We are shown to be cared for and looked out for until we stand up for the injustices done to us. Would you care to explain why our reasons behind this envy doesn't yet make sense?

A Heart

All these heartbroken people,
I envy they had a heart to begin with.
A heart to be adorned,
A heart to be tamed.

A heart to be abandoned,
A heart to be unrestrained.
All these heartbroken people,
I envy they had a love to begin with.

Despise

I despise how the moon doesn't shine
as bright without you being by my side.
You are the world I would never forget.
You are the world I would die for again.
You are my song that thunders for the sky.
With those wings you have, to be gone –
oh, how I despise that my birds
in this world don't fly that high.
I despise how you are my world but I,
I belong to a world that's so far behind.

Once you're used to getting hurt, there's nothing in this world that could bother you enough to change yourself.

Bystander

How does one reconcile
sacred will with evil?
Should one be involved
or just stand aside?
Should one protest
Or pass by the other side?

Ludicrously enough,
I'm missing what I'm most afraid of —
a sign that now… *I am safe.*

Claimed

You say I'm meant to be yours,
but I'm not a thing to be claimed
just whenever you're bored.

You say I'm meant to be yours,
but I'm not a thing to claim and use
for others to mock, envy and abuse.

You say I'm meant to be yours,
but I'm not yours to be claimed
just until you decide to leave me defamed.

Women had been kept away from the spotlight for ages and centuries; but now that they're getting that back, everyone seems to be pissed off. Sure, articles titled like *"Most powerful female CEOs of the decade"*, or *"Top law-firms run by women"*, wouldn't seem as to being given the spotlight if females were treated equally since the beginning.

Human & Woman

How much of a woman
must I be to be
even considered a human?
And how much of a human
must you be to be
considered a real man?
Why should I put in
my effort to be perfect
when you don't turn out
to be any different?

"And there I felt the second slap push me down to the floor. Nothing beats that feeling — the feeling of burning down the entire world, the feeling of wanting to be the strongest no matter what, the feeling of vengeance followed by all these wars — nothing more encouraged me than seeing my skin turn violet."

NOBODIES

Blueberries

Maybe they sent you back to my fallen self
in one more dreary attempt to calm me down.
But last winter when I looked at you,
all my eyes perceived was watching myself drown.

Patched tints of blueberries on my skin that survived —
that's how I found myself in the mirror unprepared
to encounter someone who's distorted and troubled.
And just as any other hemisphere that I faced for you,
the pieces still stubbornly attain to keep me puzzled.

Look at you, for another winter you made me return to
relearn how I struggle to align my disintegrated pieces.
I should have asked why you avoided my eyes
to just pace your own on that cobbled path below.

Instead, I've absurdly given another chance
for your friends to glare out the last air in me.
Instead, I've just given myself another scope
to lock these choke-holding tears inside of me.

This winter you dare to walk by me with a culprit face,
but don't stop there because you won't ever hear
'You're not the one to blame.' When in fact you are.
'I'm sorry' – if that's what you await, then hold on.
I'm sorry, for you, I immured the tears that tore me apart.
I'm sorry, I let you cause me this immense heartache.
I'm sorry, for your guilty pleasure I've bruised my heart.

Hold yourself tight in place, for unlike last winter
my bruises won't reappear for you to watch.
This season you will only catch the sight of a fallen
nobody soar up to a sky where a golden warmth lingers.

Misled Delusions

Not understanding
each other since the beginning
made us think our love was
"unique".

But in reality,
the realisation had come
too late that we were simply
nobodies misled into being
misplaced.

How easily misled we get,
us delusional humans…
how easily misled we get
by conditioning our minds to think,
finding an '*opposite*'
is what we must need.

Musical Chairs

First day of another year, and there we were as the last remaining pair… coincidentally, among a room full of odds. Round and round we chased around the musical chairs. There wasn't ever a way I'd compete with you, not even if it's a child's play. So, I gave in, unfocused and slow, I gave in waiting for you to make the winning move, and for me to lose more than just a game.

Gone

Painting portraits
weren't my thing
        until you came along.
My brushes and palettes –
they were coloured in you.

Painting portraits
aren't my thing
        now that you're gone.
My acrylics and pastels –
they were owned by a fool.

Would You?

if we met in
another lifetime,
        would you let me
        write your feelings?

if we got caught up
in a crossfire,
        would you save
        us from burning?

It was so naive of me to hold on to you thinking
someone better wouldn't happen to me ever again.

Bitter Liquor

You knew we could have
been so much better,
only if your heart wouldn't
be wavered by her.

Now I get lost in clubs
sipping every drop of liquor,
but remembering I loved you,
tastes so much bitter.

In a world where I have everything,
I still feel the void of you.

Forever

Even if tonight the stars escape,
and in this forever
if the sky loses its light,
Remember to not regret
that this forever we wished for
only lasted this long.
Remember to not be upset for
we couldn't catch up
with the years.
What we have made of ourselves,
remember after this sunset
our forever will still live on.

I wish I hadn't always carried a paper cutter with me
with the excuse of ending all the chapters at once.

I Won't Promise

I won't promise that I'm okay but
as I had promised,
I've kept you safe.
Today your command is
to not keep you close,
and I won't; I promise.
I can't let you stay;
and I know you won't.
I promise it's okay
to leave me be, just as I am.
But I won't promise that I'm okay.
As I have promised,
I'm letting you go.
If you're lost one day,
do come back to me.
Come back; I promise,
you'll still have me.
You will; I promise
I won't let you go astray.
I promise, I won't break my
promise no matter what you say.
But I won't promise that I'm okay.

LURE

Pause & Poison

Getting split seconds closer to being nineteen:
I suffered in silence unaware of what to feel.
Still overthinking my decisions at fifteen.
Don't even understand why I'm lonely,
Or continuously failing at this life thing so miserably.

Pushing away people just because I'll get needy,
I don't want to get judged as someone clingy.
That would be the same shit I heard at thirteen!
Far ahead than some, yet still stuck in between
A crossfire of myself and who I need to be.

Should I be worried of where this life thing is taking me?
Should I blame the child who had fell into traps so easily?
Maybe that child is just learning to love me,
But how do I love her who had constantly killed me?

This life thing really needed a Time Machine:
Pause and expose of someone who was a toxin.
I could have stopped the venom at its origin.
Or warn that kid to not get slashed by the poison,
Don't get lured into a serpent more than two times a dozen!

This life thing really needed a Time Machine:
Pause and dispose of the people I shouldn't have been.
Or at least, stop that child from becoming a ruin.
Tell her she had been drowning since the beginning.
I'm closer to being nineteen, and that's all I have seen.

Nostalgia

Nostalgia shouldn't be
suffocating me like this.

For every breath
I steal to be alive,
I feel myself being
consumed with guilt.

Nostalgia shouldn't leave
me to be tarnished like this.

For every time
I take myself home,
I sense those traps still
diffused within the air.

After all the violence I went through, I had two choices:
be gentle or be cruel.
Now, all I wish is to be gentle with myself.

Bathed in Blood

Once in a hell
without a love for myself,
I used to be the sufferer of unreasonable
consequences from conversations
that never took place.

With your love I had been
beaten, broken, torn apart, lashed,
and bathed in blood —
as if a worser hell had returned
to me from where I had left it off.

You gamble with my heart as if it's only worth
something when it belongs to anyone but me.

Flutter

I only see butterflies
in my shadow swarmed
into a fatal flutter
before they scatter
away to save each soul.

Has all the kindness really led me to this? Or is it because of all those times that I had been unkind? But even if I look back, the only person I recall being cruelly unkind to is me.

Nuisance

She's been a nuisance to some,
yet unspoken to most.
What she tenderly held within was
a promise to be less burdensome.
She's imprisoned in a paper cage,
unseen like a bewildered ghost.
If she's unspoken to you,
she's unspoken to herself too.

Home

For what home has been to me,
I hope a person never feels
like that home to me.

For what home has made of me,
I hope that person believes
how home isn't where I loved to be.

For what home has done to me,
I hope that person feels
everything but home to me.

INGROWN

Graveyard Garden

"Boy, let those smaller ones grow farther away."

"Yes, Sir." For another day I watched him being commanded by my father; they were busy renovating our garden. Not so many days ago, this part of it was just a grey graveyard of dead branches roofed by an overshadowing oak.

"Do you know the basics of gardening, boy?", father asked him as he had picked the scarlet-sprayed thorny bush. "I do, Sir.", that's all he had to say before being showered with the knowledge he never asked for. Oaks are generally exceptionally large, ours particularly held its ground for over three generations. It had so skilfully designed itself as a roof, "…it stood there just to protect the little ones…" my father said. No one dared to slice through its overgrowing roots.

"But sir, aren't all the plants here dead just because of being protected for too long?"

"They are." One after another, they picked crisp dried branches which were abandoned by the oak over the years. Beneath them were some of those 'little ones', truly a graveyard of them. He tried to save one with the support of a twig, but my father noticed and crushed it right there. I know he wanted to ask him why he killed it, and my father knew it too. "Don't give it false hope, boy. I thought you were a smart one."

"Sir, it had the power to fight, and probably survive.", he pointed at the now-diminished seedling that had successfully sprouted from beneath the heaviest of the branches.

All of a sudden, we felt the earth tremble, it was nothing but a bulky bag of fertiliser my father had dropped. "Are you not going against your own words, boy?", father referred to the question he was asked earlier.

"But sir, it's not really a garden if it fails to show us all the stages of life."

"This garden you see has a conservative mind, kid." New adults like us could barely connect 'conservative' to politics; a garden with a mind of being conservative, how could that possibly make sense? "Why do you kids think we kept this tree even though we clearly see it as an obstacle?" First, we looked up at the tree and then at each other, then cluelessly at my father.

"The area of earth this oak roof and roots on, is the driest of all the soil we see. The further we step out of its shadow, the healthier the garden seems. Every now and then it breaks off one of its own branches to keep away anyone from sprouting on the wrong grounds.

"It survives to protect and warn the little ones. It's been through all the stages of life thrice, just to give the others a better beginning. If there is a better option given to you, why would you suffer from the same consequences?"

Evergreen

How selfless must one be
to be the first one to push away
others before they begin to hurt.

How tough must one be
to keep their heart enclosed
even if it burns through their veins.

How lonely must one feel
to be the only barren one
on the land of the evergreen.

72 hours before I turn another year older, "Oh it's becoming unbearable! You and your life are giving me hell!", a few unthought words were thrown at me. Nothing really happened. I just stayed silent as usual, while the last strings of the little child in me suddenly got snatched away. Just like that, I must now be able to bear all the hurtful words people throw at me, after all I'm almost 20 now. The less I ask for, the lesser I'm given. The lesser I'm given, the more I listen. The more I listen, the greater I break. If only you could walk by all the hells I'm going through, I wonder, if you would have the courage to break me like that again.

Homeland

Evergreen, but momentarily alive
is this skin that hugs me tight.
Beneath this ever-changing surface
that might once loose its foliage,
it goes through endless seasons
and infinite revolutions.
My skin – the ruins of
a battlefield, and a *homeland*.

She used to be the happiest soul to walk over these lands which were once a warm blooming field of the yellow suns – the *Lady of Sorrows*, was her name. The story behind her oddly conflicting name had begun when she grew afraid of losing her flowers to native birds who fed on their seeds; and to keep herself from losing her most adorned possession she decided to cut off the entire field within blooming season — the way she could have all her flowers under her protection, without the fear of any sparrows. Once, twice, thrice, and again… she continued without realising that even the very thing that symbolises longevity could lose its own life; she plucked them all until her field never grew again. Little did she know, her greed for saving all the happiness for herself – which she believed was only her loyalty to those sunflowers – would make her lands barren, scarce, and die of thirst for the sun which waits for the call of sparrows to announce its rise. *The Lady of Sorrows lost to a flock of sparrows.*

World of Fragments

When the clouds roar,
rain is a song of sadness.
Every fragment of this world is
inevitable to fall into a decoy.

When the rain drops,
earth rhythms a song of joy.
Every fragment of this world is
bound to be found by its happiness.

We all reach for the sky ignoring that the ground has been holding us close to all that we have.

People never really grow up. They're just children stuck within a messed-up reality forced to look like they understand exactly how the world works.

Erudition

A forest should be pretty,
shouldn't it?
With all its hues of green
and shades of liveliness,
with all its tones and tunes
for melodising its existence —
a forest must be pretty,
mustn't it?
But a season where
it only briefly exists,
and even at nights when
it silents down to rest,
a forest can only
look pretty to a few at best.
A forest can be pretty;
just feel the depths of it.

ENEMIES

Save Your Sacrifices

When I think back to that morning of nineteen-sixty-three's gore summer where it all began to end, the daybreak was gore not only because of the south's unbearable humidity, but much worse because of the human landfills of a city we were surrounded by. Thankfully, being an employee of the avidly named *Commoners' Care Shelter* under the British rule, I wouldn't have to step out of the shelter to watch the ravens feeding on nameless bodies. Mornings in lands of the Bengal used to commence with the simple crowing of roosters at dawn, even before the clock ticked to five.

"Five A.M sharp!", a drilling alarm stated the time throughout resident corridors intended to awake the foreign caregivers and doctors; me being the only local practitioner howsoever, needn't such a method. My first day on that base reflected upon me as I had gradually paced through the *Hall of Ravens* for the commencement of yet another day of unsuccessful treatments. What an extraordinary museum it was — displaying bleak works of black and white paintings by renowned artists who had been inspired from the outcome of their own leader's cruelties — the *Hall of Ravens* was nothing, but a graveyard trapped in frames and a memory of my worst enemy.

About forty-five years ago that day, I met a man in blue; had I known that would be the only and last of his essence, I wouldn't agree to wear the ring I still have on until today. It rather remains as a picture of black and white for today's world of modernism though. *Or should I begin like this?* Almost half a century ago, I met him at museum of colourless ravens, and until today his lifelike presence has been stuck in my mind like a contemporary painting. *"Save your sacrifices."*, were the last of his words I heard while being faced to his back on that hall. A man so stern and true to his words, without even looking back at me for one last glimpse of affection, he willingly gave up a life with his fiancé of just three-days for war. A war that led to the making of at least a thousand more paintings of those colourless ravens, still prized by today's artists.

Though it had been months since I battled my way into this base to serve my own people, I was only able to watch them being starved to death. Malaria, flu, injuries — I was capable of curing; but a famine caused by the rage of war authorities and not droughts? I didn't hold the power to treat them. Only the ravens who fed on the dead, and terrorisers in positions of power remained satisfied with an overfilled stomach.

"I never told you to fall in love with me,
it's all on you."

Enemy

I'm the worst person you could ever meet.
I can make you fall apart
        or make you fall in love
all within a matter of a few twisted words.

I'm the worst person you could ever meet.
I can leave you to the wolves
        or carry you over broken glass
just to show you, to me what you're worth.

Never make a deal with anyone you know,
you're going to be at a disadvantage right away.

Why?

The night's about to end
but I'm soaked in sweat.
I can't say why; I don't know why.
Life is tough, you know for sure
but can't you let me breathe a little while?
The human in me, it's about to die.
In the middle of the day,
I'm caught in dreams.
I can't say why, I don't know why.
Fake friends… they all lie.
Falling for enemies,
being buried in books and series –
they're only things that make me high.
Being too honest doesn't seem right,
and being too secretive, for what?
I don't know why; I can't say why.

"My favourite colours were black and blue,
until they turned into the bruises from you."

West

Lake of the west
where the blood-bathed sun rests,
that's the place we first met –
that's the place we must forget.

Patience & Practitioner

"Are you in a relationship?", he had already indicated that at this age, as a teenager, I must have coiled myself into one, to be suddenly diagnosed with anxiety and depression. Though diagnosed out of order and later than many, mine wasn't certainly very sudden, I had known since the beginning.

The answer in my head narrated, "I'm afraid of relationships, I'm afraid of outsiders, I'm afraid of being close to new people, I'm afraid to trust people, I'm afraid of being attached.", among many others. My lips on the other hand, were still sealed together. Just nodding sideways with a smile that could deceive — the first tactic I could use to avoid a spoken answer.

"Why don't you socialise?", the practitioner continued with his interrogation, "What is it that's stopping you from meeting new people?"

"Do I really have to say all of it again?", my head screamed, "I'm afraid!" He didn't hear the voice inside. And finally, after my many attempts of dodging the tsunami of his questions, I spoke a simple sentence obscurely covering the truth: "I just don't feel like it", accompanied with an expression that I had patiently practiced a thousand times before paying him a visit.

Confidentiality between patients and practitioners may exist elsewhere, but in a country where laws and policies are practiced according to one's mood swings, even my lies with a doctor would not be protected. In a country where depression only exists as myths, children can only be blamed with unreasonable and generalised causes listed by adults who once went through the same treatment.

Flee

You can flee a war zone
after throwing the bomb.
But you can't flee an afterlife in hell.

And if you don't believe in afterlives,
then you can't escape the self-destructing
torture even if you survive that war.

When history repeats itself, from it we either learn to adapt for our betterment or we lead ourselves to a worse type of destruction; and believe it or not, this applies to both global and personal timelines.

;

Secret Keeper

At that moment we looked up at the same sky, that same moon still being indecisive of hiding behind those fleeting tear-bearers; even those stellar stars began falling. “We’re not the same if not opposites, you know?”, I uttered softly. He however, showed no sign of a response. “You see this night sky as ‘beautiful’…”, I continued. This time though, he showed a fading smile with another unspecific expression. “… I see it full of sadness and remorse, as if it’s guilty of keeping deadly secrets.”

He turned as I finished. “Do you not see me as a good secret keeper?”, the worry on his face expressed more than all he had said since nightfall. I lost all my words; me who would give life to a deteriorating rock with her words! His face went blank as he looked back upon the trembling sky. I couldn’t keep on the silence, so I spoke along the shushing wind. “You’re the only one I can’t see through. I don’t understand how—”

“To be honest, we truly are opposites standing on the same surface.”, he suddenly cut me off. I felt my heart clenching onto me. “We see things differently, but in the same complex manner.”

“Are you sure of that?”, that very instant I had turned to him. He nodded, and again with that unreadable face he turned to me. “We’re opposites in a terrifyingly similar way. And… you and I both know what’s stopping us.” I grasped onto my keys as he continued reading my mind. “We’re afraid taking that risk will eventually end us. But not taking it will end us right at this moment.”

I hesitated to reply to his words for a bit. “Should… should we seriously risk letting our guards down for ‘us’?”, my heart gradually loosened its tight grip on me. With the clanking of my keys, he held his hand on mine, “Our walls have already touched the sky; it’s better if they collapse back into earth now.” We exhaled in relief, and in terror. “You’re the best secret keeper I know.”

“I know I’m the only secret keeper you know.”, he replied. Expressing vivid emotions wasn’t the best of his talents, or so I thought. We didn’t know if it all had dawned with nightfall, but our choice was to keep going; even when that dusk disappeared.

We can be a part of each other, but we should never forget to respect the part that belongs to oneself either. Being complete was never part of the equation, what's important is how exchanging parts can make us better together.

INTO

Birdwatcher

Chimes of the watchtower rustled with the last dance of the swaying trees; it was time for the lilies and lotuses to go to sleep. I watched a heron with its feet clawed to the sweeping wet sand as it was too cautiously beaked at that dying sun which served a message for many. For the heron though, it was a call for it to soar back to its nest before the snakes slithered into those reeds.

"If you neglect your beloved for too long, they're bound to be swayed away." — is what a birdwatcher would say; stay a little longer and you too will know how birds rarely let their eggs out of sight for too long.

Into You

How do I cope with the fact that everything in the world
does matter without you?

Unknowingly, have I fallen into your simple acts?
Unknowingly, have I turned into someone else?
Unknowingly, have I given into your heart too fast?

How do I convince myself to believe that my world
shouldn't revolve around you?

Yet

You don't know it yet, but my eyes are your home, where you belong to show me a thousand dreams no matter what time of the day it is.

And I don't show it yet, but your smile is the only reason my heart beats; you are the only one who could be my vulnerability and my strength.

Yearning

This city is filled with
an overbearing scent
that almost pulls you
into its amassed crowds,

but oddly enough a scent
so powerfully petrifying
doesn't always please
one's yearning of sweetness.

Am I just in denial?
Or have I really given into you?

Blades & Chronicles

Whether blades, or just chronicles of you
They're both sharp enough to cut through
        A heart —
it's burdened with nothingness, but
leaks within to keep getting heavier.
        Draw scars —
some invisible,
others to be forgotten through the years.
Whether swords, or just chronicles of you
They're both sharp enough to cut through
        A heart —
it's almost dried out to pump,
today it beats no more
yet the end seems nowhere near.

Sometimes things go right for the **wrong** person and that's a part of life we must accept. It's the only way for us to learn and make things go right for the **right** person.

Barrels

Believe it or not, I’ve been through it all:
been a fool, feeling hollow like empty barrels.
took cautious steps just to trip into life’s pitfall
Believe it or not, for me, being anything else
would be better than being a human at all.

DEEPER

Deep Beneath

I closed my eyes and jumped off. But a sudden instinct made me grab onto a tiny twig-like branch. All the heaviness of the thoughts which made me take that decision, were weighing down to my feet. I hear a crack. Is this it? — I ask myself. Is this how you want to regret your life? — I ask myself again, then a second crack follows. I don't dare to look down; not yet. But I looked up to where I stood before. If I was so ready to jump, why had I closed my eyes? If I were to end it here, why am I holding on to something so weak? If I don't care to see myself up there again, why do I fear what's beneath? I hear the third and final crack; it's time. And my eyes are wide open now. Sleep tight, little one; you've healed from those nights.

Deeply Shallow

My heart all of a sudden felt bound to be hollow. And though it never deeply held any name, it still felt passively betrayed. I had told myself, "Don't go any deeper!", "Don't fall too deep!", "Don't think too deeply!", but who would listen?

Deeper – a word with indefinite depth, but it left me to become shallow.

If I had known you would eventually leave,
why would I ever choose to fall so deep?

Nothingness

Why do I have everything?
But nothing.
Am I insane?
Probably not.
It's all just in my head.
Do I cry myself to sleep?
Not really,
it's just the tears tracing down
my skin that keeps me awake.
Do I care about others?
A bit too much.
Do I care about myself?
A bit too less.
Deep down, am I just broken?
Maybe, like everyone else.
All I have is nothingness,
but why do I feel everything?

We're reading the same words,
but we aren't on the same page.

Once Again II

Once again, but just one last time
we flew in opposite directions.
Once and for all, we flew the furthest
just to live with our recollections.

Some parents tend to force their own failures onto their children expecting to witness a victory they couldn't achieve themselves. And later it gets to be romanticised for making up heroic stories behind their successes. Or if occurs otherwise as the same old conclusion, it is passed on to the ones next in line.

Stop

For you and I,
the world wouldn't stop.
For the world,
you and I shouldn't stop.

Oasis

At a time where everyone races to express their individuality louder than ever, something powerfully invisible remains stubbornly constant within us all. *Loneliness*. It's ironic how we try to grab attention and affection through portraying our uniqueness, yet that very thing is what drives us deeper into the pit we're running from. Could there ever be an oasis between individuality and unity?

I'm drunk, so drunk that I tasted the flavours of a
vineyard of your passion ageing centuries within me.

Cassias

I miss it. How do I make the world comprehend? I miss spring. The feverishness of a rubescent perfume fused with the air that glides over new leaves, the exotic calls of foreign birds celebrating a new beginning, the bizarre paintings of the sky curated by every springtide evening — I outrageously miss it all.

But it is the spring which hasn't happened to me yet that I speak of, I'm heavily longing for the time that hasn't become. How do I make them believe that deep down I'm nostalgic about the purging cassias which haven't bloomed for the new arrival of another young summer?

Would you believe if I said that deep in my past, none of my spring times were meant to be missed? So far in my future I'm still waiting for a spring that I'm nostalgic of.

IMPURITIES,

Sometimes I forget I'm still breathing. All it takes is a single tiny trigger to take me back. Or should I say remind me of where I'm stuck? Years ago, with my head down on my knees, deep beneath a tiny dug out burrow. And me? I was even tinier than that. It was too hard to breathe. Holding myself down with a string clutched among my fingers. Lady of the night had begun to bloom, an invitation sent for the snakes. But I wasn't afraid of their poison; I wished they would get to me before that demonised figure did. A broken kite was all that was left of me, just like the one that flew away leaving me with its string. And again, I tried to hold onto that string… even that string I held onto, ended up being the very thing to cut through my bones.

Hide & Seek

I'm here.
Six years later.
Six feet away.
He's there.
Six years later.
Still the same,
Impure,
I'm scared.
Terrified,
Still in the past.
He's cruel,
Ecstatic,
Of that age.
I had been
Haunted,
Hunted.
He was the
Hunter.
It was not just
Hide and seek.

He sought,
I hid.
He said,
I obeyed.
The wrong places,
Touched.
Pushed.
Caressed.
Bruised.
I'm here, again.
Six thousand voices
That screamed to
Just stay away.
I'm here.
He's there.
Just six feet away.
Like a mirror of
The past,
That had just begun
To fade away.

Netherworld

Eyes burn as if they belong to the netherworld, but what's within me that's hellbent on holding back my tears?

Throat is gripped on a chokehold; these chains turned into iron but not even a sip of water is borne in me.

Why do I not see the frost? Where has it disappeared? The hellfire of this world has turned me purely scarce.

Every inch of my skin – taunted with shivering chills. Not a drip of rain, not a flake of snow, and barely a life left to show.

Silent Night

Will this night never stop talking?
Until yesterday,
all it did was consume
my mind with its silence.

Will this war ever turn to be chaste?
This silence of the night is
fiddled over these bamboo roofs:
it gets louder, noisier, filthier.

One's long held purity gets hidden with dirt.
One's brief purity covers the dirt.
How we may be deceived
relies entirely on how we perceive.

Hyacinths

Blankets and scents that lie around here,
Reminds me a past that I don’t want to hear.
Souls and memories that died around here –
hyacinths bloom from them yet the sky’s never clear.

How should I tell them I'm no fighter, and
yet stains of blood are the least of my fears?

Dirty Mirror

I've trained myself not to be
too expressive with my emotions —
the sole reason why others
find me intimidating.
But with this one person sat
on the other side of the room,
I can't help myself from losing it all.
I sit here all day looking
at the dirty mirror and
I lose it all when I'm unable to
find a spot on that surface reflecting me;
all the dirt that I see is on me.
I've washed myself from
one sunrise to another dawn,
I've scrubbed myself
until my skin had blisters
to lessen the pain of this dirt,
yet it's stubbornly marked on me.
I've trained myself to be stern,
I've trained myself to be nicer,
but with this person on the mirror
I can't help but lose it all.

How frightened do you have to be to lose sleep over a devilish scent which is far gone with the winds?

Protector

While playing with my kite which struggled to fly for that windless summer afternoon, I had bumped into a figure triple my height. He wore a uniform and a badge that represented the protectors of civilians. It was the second time he visited that weekend.

"How old are you turning next week?" he asked leaning down to me.

"Nine.", I replied naively.

"Leave your kite here. It's getting dark, let's go inside."

"But I want to play more."

"You know it's my duty to protect all civilians. Let's go and I will show you something you've never seen before."

I followed him back to our guest hall.

"If you want to play, promise me you will keep this a secret. Okay?"

"Does my mother know?", she must know – I thought.

"No, it's just going to be between us."

I nodded believing he'll show me the secret of how he heroically saves people from danger. But it wasn't *that* secret of his which he showed me, and neither was it a secret to be known by children. Whatever I had seen that evening, I couldn't bring the words at that time even if I wanted to tell someone. And that incompetence of me trapped me further into getting unwillingly involved.

By the time I finally learnt the words to describe what he had done throughout years, I realised none of what I say would be believed anymore. Even now that it has been several more years since I left my kite in that cruel place which I called home, there's a question that still keeps me up at night – *are children supposed to know how to protect themselves from those who are called the protectors of this world?*

DON'T THEY?

Children Lie

I lied.

Those times when I stole one more lollipop from the pantry; you kept it at a height I could reach too easily. Those times when I stole your makeup; I wanted to look like you. Those times I stole from your closet when I wanted to be like a princess ornamented with your jewellery and draped with your wedding dress thrice the size of me.

The times I lied, you let me go without a word. But that once, when I was my most brave and sincere self, when I needed you to hold me, console me, protect me, you didn't let it go without my death. Maybe physically I'll still breathe, but the only feeling I'll ever feel is of the wreathed dead. But I don't want to blame you as my last goodbye. So, I'll accept your accusations — children lie, don't they? I did…

I lied.

Kite

I used that kite as my shield
but it trapped me in its string.
Bones of it remained still as steel,
but none of mine are left to being.

Of course, a stranger will treat you better than me. They don't know how you're going to ruin their life, do they?

She Knew

My mother doesn't exactly know why I turned out to be the one she describes to others. Sometimes, I'm not even sure whether I should be concerned or relieved that she hasn't forced me to know more. At times I question myself whether she realises how cruelly precise her way of describing her child is:

"She is among those people who would not shed a single tear in front of anyone even if her pain makes her loose her existence to the oblivion inside." What made her capture such a feature of me?

"Even if her knees are forcing her down to the ground, she will remain still until there's no one to watch her break apart into pieces." Did she watch me without my knowledge?

"She never cries, at least I haven't seen her do that in years." What was the last reason she saw me crying for? Mothers know their children the best, don't they? Some know by trying their best for their child, while others get to know unwillingly and unprepared. And some are just hanging in between. Mine tried to know until I closed myself off not too long ago; however, even then she knew everything. Maybe she observed, or maybe she presumed, but her words whispered *she knew*.

"The decisions we make as kids, shape how successful we become as adults", that's what I've been told my entire life. But why isn't anyone interested in understanding that the way we get hurt as children make the type of adults we become? Could that be or not be what leads us to live as a successful human?

From a Griever

"Children lie; don't they?", her voice broke before continuing what was left off unfinished, "I did…" That morning, the monsoon rain stopped pouring, and birds thereafter never stopped mourning.

Would it be any different if that dawn never broke its silence? Only if I could say I believed her. That I trusted her with every one of those words she had gathered up the courage to tell me, I wouldn't be grieving today. The most rarely spoken issues tend to go nameless among the crowd of the famed though those are the ones requiring the much-needed attention.

"Liar, liar pencil on fire." – it's time to hold a pen.

Lies of Love

I lied,
not from the beginning
but until the end,
I lied.
I loved,
not until the end
but from the beginning,
I loved.

It might not entirely be known to the world, but there are children who have led a double life since they found societal exposure. At times they're someone when they are out there, and at times they're someone they aren't when they are home; and in between being exhausted to lead those contradicting selves, they've already lost their true self. Who should they be when everyone they have been isn't at all a person recognisable to them?

Farewell

My lies depicted
all the truths
I could never tell,
and they foreshadow
all that I am
as I say *farewell*.

Some of us are just repeating generations, reforming what has been witnessed several times, reinventing the obvious one more time; some of us are just living as the ones who we loved first by continuously resenting what they have done.

•

I've Become a Bride

I've become everything — a wife, a mother, a daughter, an uninvited member of another family, a defamed woman and a runaway bride who never dared to run away. My name follows such rumours as I've achieved to become everything, but a bride. If I was ever given the chance to change my past, would I?

No, I wouldn't change a thing I did, nor would I run; but I do consider changing my parents' past if I did have the power. I know my parents were a lot less brave as children, and once at their time as teenagers when they were also a bride and a groom.

It takes a lot for a child to turn out to be different from what their parents were; many understandably do not go to such painful extents just to be a few further circumstances better.

So, if I had the power to change the past, I wish I could do that for them. Nevertheless, just as they have served their time in this abyss of a cell, I too have become nothing but an unescaped criminal convicted of dehumanising myself.

•

I don't want to end this conversation here, but time's running out and I've got a kite to catch; don't let yours loose its way pacing through the scrolling winds.

Go ahead. Even if it's exhausting to be this honest about what you've been through, pour your heart out, I promise it's alright here.

AFTERWORD

"That string I held onto ended up being the very thing to cut through my bones."

Children Lie; I Did..., being the third book and second poetry collection under my belt, is my most unguarded and raw possession. Never forget to remember: No matter who or where you are, and with everything that you have been through, you will be loved and understood by someone out there – way more than you could ever manage to do yourself; otherwise, you yourself are enough too.

I am unquestionably, both terrified and excited to share this collection with the world; and regardless of the nervousness I feel, I would definitely love to see how you relate to the pieces it holds. Therefore, please do reach out; don't hesitate even if it's just to have a little uplifting chat.

@mehjabin.prova (Instagram & TikTok), @mehjabin_prova (Twitter), @mehjabinprova (YouTube)

Or e-mail me at oeuvre.publications@gmail.com I will definitely read and reply to every one of them.

ACKNOWLEDGEMENT

Thank you. Thank you so much for everything — this is coming sincerely from a heart filled with adoration, respect and encouragement for you.

Thank you. Thank you to everyone who have been here since the beginning of *Sonnets of the Scarlette Sea* and *Seasons of Desire*; my *Sasakia* butterflies who have encouraged me since day one, you all are so, so precious.

Thank you. Thank you to the ones who have just joined our new beginning; don't worry, history can be read if you haven't lived it. Please do consider becoming a part of our flutter of *Sasakias*. We don't discriminate.

And I'll say this again: At the end of every beginning, **you** are still the reason why you should keep on living.

Until our next beginning,
Mehjabin H. Prova

ABOUT THE AUTHOR

Mehjabin Hossain Prova, commonly known as Prova, is a Bangladeshi-Portuguese debut author and poet of the poetry collection, *Sonnets of the Scarlette Sea*, and script novel series, *Seasons of Desire.* Born in Dhaka, Bangladesh, she moved to Portugal after completing her primary education. Though Prova has always been recalled as the 'quiet', 'shy', and sometimes even an 'intimidating' girl back in her childhood, her days were mostly spent either in solitude or writing away whatever had come to mind with every passing moment. Her first ever poem, or piece of personal writing can be traced back to when she was just eleven; triggered by a time which had brought drastic changes into her life. But with that time, not only she has matured with age, but also with her writing.

Just before Prova graduated high school, she decided to form a full collection of all that she had written throughout the years, however, with much more professionalism and profoundness since publishing her works was one of her other-worldly dreams. *Seasons of Desire*, on the other hand, is an openly popular script novel series with *'The Encounter'* completed as its first season; it is said to be continued without any fixed release dates. Currently, Prova has been enrolled in university to continue her studies after she spent a gap-year to travel, spend more time reflecting on herself, explore her roots, and work on her upcoming poetry collection dated to be released by 2022.

BOOKS BY THIS AUTHOR:

Poetry:

Sonnets of the Scarlette Sea
(https://www.amazon.com/dp/B09MYXXH3S)

Novel:

Seasons of Desire: The Encounter
(Original Script Version)
(https://www.amazon.com/dp/B09MYRBG14)

Sources:
Google: https://g.co/kgs/KXvWBn
About: https://www.amazon.com/author/mehjabin.prova
SNS: https://www.instagram.com/mehjabin.prova/
YouTube: https://www.youtube.com/mehjabinprova/

www.ingramcontent.com/pod-product-compliance
Lightning Source LLC
LaVergne TN
LVHW091317150826
845673LV00006B/1676

* 9 7 9 8 3 6 7 9 3 4 1 6 8 *